From Sorrows to Glory

Mary Helen Lopez

TRILOGY CHRISTIAN PUBLISHERS

TUSTIN, CA

Trilogy Christian Publishers
A Wholly Owned Subsidiary of Trinity Broadcasting Network
2442 Michelle Drive
Tustin, CA 92780

From Sorrows to Glory

Trilogy Christian Publishers A Wholly Owned Subsidiary of Trinity Broadcasting Network

2442 Michelle Drive Tustin, CA 92780

Cover design by Jeff Summers

For information about special discounts for bulk purchases, please contact Trilogy Christian Publishing.

Manufactured in the United States of America

10 9 8 7 6 5 4 3 2 1

Library of Congress Cataloging-in-Publication Data is available.

ISBN: 978-1-63769-978-2

E-ISBN: 978-1-63769-979-9

This book is dedicated to the God of Abraham, Isaac, and Jacob, for He has revealed His love toward us from times past to present. To the Son Jesus Christ for His obedience to the Father and for making a way for us to live with Him forever. To the Holy Spirit for teaching us, helping us, comforting us, and for being the very best friend that anyone can ever have.

Contents

Introduction

As much as I tried, I couldn't refrain from disclosing the once upon a time secrets and the sad memories I had—the painful and shameful areas of life that we would rather not share with others, which many out there would agree are not things that we like to talk about, much less write about, especially in detail. Nevertheless, God had a different plan regarding this book—a plan that He, my pain, and my shame, and through the work of the Holy Spirit, would reveal who He is, His unconditional love, and how He moves in a person's life to set them free in a most distinct way. I would have to expose all the painful and shameful circumstances that took a toll on my life to the point of death. What Jesus was asking of me brought on hours of pain and tears in front of my old faithful computer. Therefore, I proceeded courageously and joined the Almighty God, the Son, and the Holy Spirit in the blueprint He designed for this book.

The beginning of this book started with one leaf of paper that I had written while I was incarcerated back in 1999. I ran across this one page that I had placed in a folder, along with other papers that I felt were important, in a box that I had stored in my mother's shed. This folder remained in that box and in that shed for many years. It was not until seven years ago that I yielded to the leading of the Holy Spirit and began the process of sharing with the world the hidden, painful, and shameful memories of my life. When I started writing, there were mountains—mountains that were too big for me to handle—mountains high and wide that elevated from the depths of darkness; they were placed in my path to stop the manifestation of what God had planned. In the process, I experienced physical complications and emotional distress, but through God's grace, mercy, and the power of His Word, I overcame.

> And Jesus answered saying to them, "Have faith in God. "Truly I say to you, whoever says to this mountain, 'Be taken up and cast into the sea,' and does not doubt in his heart, but believes that what he says is going to happen, it shall be granted him."
> Mark 11:22–23

The mountains were lifted and were thrown into the sea, and I continued to proceed forward, with boldness and without hesitation. The truth began to manifest in ways that I never had imagined. Thoughts of how vital this information would be for others opened my mind to the many lives that would be changed and to the expansion of my Father's kingdom. For this book to be effective, I stood on two scriptures, "I can do all things through Him who strengthens me" (Philippians 4:13), and "So shall my word be which goes forth from My mouth; it shall not return to Me empty, Without accomplishing what I desire, And without succeeding in the matter for which I sent it" (Isaiah 55:11).

I submitted to His will, and was obedient to His direction, and did exactly what my Father asked of me.

Pain and shame are just two of Satan's sharpest tools in that shed of his and have affected multiple upon multiples of individuals—the innocent and the not so innocent, the strong and the weak, the rich and the poor; the brown, black, and the white. For thousands of years, all of mankind has had their share of Satan's evil materials and plans. I pray that this book draws millions of lost souls into God's kingdom, I pray that it reaches those who are in bondage to evil roots from infancy to adulthood and that it sets free those with uncontrollable addictions—addictions that, from times past, have carried with them factors that have actively contributed to heartbreaking and devastating situations. Satan's tools are out to destroy God's children, and I was one of them.

Little Mary Helen

I can still recall the emptiness that had lingered within me after so many years. I remember I was only seven years old, standing in front of my grandparent's house one night, looking up into the night sky, acknowledging how high and wide the sky was; the many stars, the bright moon, and the sadness that filled my heart, just knowing that I would never see my dad again. It was a time of great emotional pain for me. It was the spring of 1963, in a place called Barstow, a small town on the southeast part of California, a place where I was surrounded by my parents' and grandparents' love and security. I was the eldest of four children and was loved by my family dearly.

On the morning of May 10th, I was instructed by my mother to go half day to school and come home; I was to accompany her and my dad to a certain hospital in San Bernardino, California, where my mother thought that my father would receive the help he needed for his restlessness and the abuse of alcohol. My dad served in the Army, in the 15th Armored Infantry Battalion in Korea, in which he was a corporal, a few weeks shy of becoming a sergeant. He, instead, decided to come home because he missed my mom. When he was honorably discharged, he was not the same, as I was told by my mother. We believe now that the reason for the change in my dad was due to both PTSD and witchcraft, which, back then in the '60s, PTSD was not acknowledged, not as much as it is now. On the other hand, witchcraft has been around for thousands of years; it is a practice that has been very well known to all humanity and can be highly effective when jealousy, hatred, and covetousness have their way. Our Father in heaven will have no part in this type of evil behavior.

There shall not be found among you anyone who makes his son or his daughter pass through the fire, one who uses divination, one who practices witchcraft, or one who interprets omens, or a sorcerer, or one who casts a spell, or a medium, or a spiritist, or one who calls up the dead.

Deuteronomy 18:10–11

Witchcraft and PTSD were the major causes for my dad's actions. He would drink heavily to relieve the symptoms of the spell, which was so intense, and for the disorder of PTSD—the combination of both caused evil hallucinations and aggressiveness. My mother was incognizant, and back then, the leading of the Holy Spirit was not present, there was no "Let us go to church, so they can pray for you," there was no "Let us pray and ask Jesus to help you," the wisdom of the world was all that we could count on, which meant being defeated and without hope—without Jesus, there is no hope. "Remember that you were at that time separated from Christ, excluded from the commonwealth of Israel, and strangers to the covenants of promise, having no hope and without God in the world" (Ephesians 2:12). Therefore, the thought of my dad being set free from this bondage was never resolved or mentioned because the house we lived in was built on sand; we did not have a firm foundation (Matthew 7:24–27), and because of this, little did we know, this house was about to all come crumbling down. We did not know Jesus the way we know Him now. My mother has admitted many times, "If I would've known the Lord the way I know Him now, this never would've happened." That is why many pastors and believers stress the issue of staying in tune with God's Word because God's Word brings you to a place where you know exactly where you stand in His kingdom, acknowledging the power that we have. "Behold, I have given you authority to tread upon serpents and scorpions, and over all the power of the enemy, and nothing shall injure you" (Luke 10:19).

Unfortunately, when I made my way home from school at noontime, it was too late. I heard all this crying coming from inside my grandparents' house—a day that I guess I will never forget. I remember, as I entered the little gate, my neighbor Kenneth, who was younger than I, approached me and said, "Your daddy is dead." I stood there just looking at him; I could not, for that moment, understand why he would say something like this to me. Even though I heard the crying, I was not accepting it. As I made my way into the house, I naturally looked directly where my mother was and saw many, many tears rolling down her face; it was true, my dad had done something to himself. I found out many years later that it was called "suicide," he had committed suicide. We, today, can only assume that he arrived at this decision because of the emotional state he was in and could not bear it any longer; therefore, he felt there was no other way out but to take his own life. My dad was suffering, and no one at that time realized just how much. This type of suffering recalls a scripture that says, "Constantly, night and day, among the tombs and in the mountains, he was crying out and gashing himself with stones" (Mark 5:5). My dad was desperate.

When I got older and put all the pieces together, I felt like a coward. It was at that moment when the guilt of not being there to stop him got the best of me.

At an incredibly young age, I learned to put up my guard. My whole world was turned upside down. From being a child, who was under her dad's strict authority, I was now a menace. I became rebellious, full of bitterness and anger. My dad left me, and I just could not get over it, especially because I was awfully close to my dad. This was just the beginning of sorrows for me. Little did I know, then, that the same way our Heavenly Father has a plan for our lives, the enemy has a plan too—a plan to destroy us. I, of course, did not have a clue, then, what was about to happen to me—my life would be changed immensely. More then than ever, I had become open prey for Satan and all his works of evil.

Sexual Immorality

Sexual molestation was waiting for me right outside my front door. Now, as an adult, when I watch the news or I hear about someone becoming a victim of sexual abuse or human trafficking, it's a hard thing for me to accept as part of this life, and it's especially harder for me to admit that it happened to me. The thought of being sexually molested—and the effects of that experience—has had a great impact on my life. It was May of 1963 when my dad left, and it was August of 1963, at a downtown theatre, in this small town in Southeastern California, that the molestation began. I can still remember a sense of weakness and shame flooding my inner-being. Even though I was a child, I knew that what had just happened was wrong, but because of the shame, I never told anyone. I kept it a secret until now.

When I got to this part of the book, the shame once again surfaced, and it felt awkward because I am now a new creation; I did not like having to relive this part of my life. Once again, I felt myself going back to that little hiding place that I was accustomed to; I began to pull up my guard and put the mask back on. So…I talked to the Lord Jesus about sharing this with the world and extremely dreading it. He assured me that this was necessary, that this needed to come out in the open for the purpose of drawing millions of lost souls into His kingdom. Jesus said, "You need to let all females and males, of all ages, know that there is hope and that what I have done for you, I will do for anyone who puts their trust in Me. Through your obedience, many lost souls in this evil generation will find Me, they will acknowledge Me, and I will set them free." "And you shall know the truth, and the truth shall make you free" (John 8:32).

When I was a child, my heart was wounded—the molestation had affected me deeply. I began to gradually experience intense fear and confusion, and we know that God is not a God of confusion but of peace (1 Corinthians 14:33). This trauma became too much for a child my age to be going through, much less the uncertainty of what would come next. I felt as if I was lost in my own little world because, outside of my world, everything and everyone went about doing their own thing as usual. Fear was my constant companion; I never had peace. I found out, much later in life, that the fear I was dealing with was panic attacks. From this information, I gathered that I, as a child, was not able to mentally contain the trauma that had been forced upon me, therefore, leaving me in a mental state of shock, and on my own, looking for ways to find relief from all this pain and shame.

Nevertheless, I continued to play with my brothers, with my friends and my dolls; it was as if I were trying my best to ignore it—no one had any idea what I had experienced, and because of this, there was no healing, causing roots of evil in my soul that would grow into many hardships in the years to follow. My mother—the virtuous woman (Proverbs 31)—was always there; she always made sure that I was very well taken care of, and her support was the best that a child could ever ask for, but the self-blame and the shame kept me from telling her about the sexual molestation, along with the fear of what she would think of me and what she would say. But, when it comes to God's children, God says, "Do not fear, for I am with you; Do not anxiously look about you, for I am your God. I will strengthen you, surely I will help you, Surely I will uphold you with My righteous right hand" (Isaiah 41:10).

I was a child who had experienced a part of life that I knew nothing about, except for the reality of mixed emotions and a wrongdoing that completely took over—a stronghold that was more powerful than I and would not let go of me. I was out of control; this alone brought on all the dishonorable and improper reasons that kept me in a dark place for such a long time. As life went on, I was not only dealing with the death of my dad but now the effects of physical sexual molestation. But…there was something else connected to the sensual immorality that I had been coerced to endure; this was happening at night as I slept. Whether it was psychological or spiritual, I cannot say, but this experience was strange. I would put my head on my pillow at bedtime, and as I wandered off to sleep, I would feel this person—I am saying it was a man. In my dream or vision, he never once let me see his face—if I turned to the left or the right, he would always stay behind me. It was a slender man of a tall, structured body; he would caress me like what appeared to be someone or something who was lonely and needed someone to comfort him. He stayed close, but he never attempted to go further than that and would proceed to hold me until I would awaken.

Was it the enemy, causing more havoc, or was it me crying out, even in my dreams? Because this happened more than once, it continued throughout all my childhood, teenage years, and part of my adult life. In every episode, I felt an intense fear that would proceed to bring me to a state of curiosity about who or what this person was and what was the purpose? It is still a mystery. This also was something else that I never shared with anyone because I felt that if I had said something concerning this encounter, I would never have a definite answer on exactly who or what this person or spirit was. The only one I know now who could answer this question and many other questions that I had and still have would be Jesus, the omniscient Savior. He knows why these dreams were repetitive and mysterious. Or can it be, as it says in God's Word, "For in many dreams and in many words there is emptiness. Rather, fear God" (Ecclesiastes 5:7). In other words, do not fear the unknown, do not pay attention to dreams or visions where the questions and answers that you seek are to no avail. Instead, fear God, respect Him, stay close to Him and His Word. Worship Him daily, in spirit and in truth, and He will always be there for you.

I was carrying a heavy load and needed so bad to be set free. I did not even have peace in my dreams; it was like my life, from an incredibly young age, was evolved around sexual immorality—born to be sexually used and abused, a burden that followed me every day of my life. This tedious journey brought on frustration and anger, which I gradually turned inwards.

In 1966, we moved here, to Albuquerque, New Mexico; it became so hard for me to relocate; after all, I had just come from attending St. Joseph's Catholic School in California, and now a public school. Over there, the teachers were nuns, and here, the teachers were teachers; it just was not the same, but then again, it did not matter what I did or where I went, I always felt this emptiness—an emptiness that I learned, in such a hard way, that this world could not satisfy; only Jesus could satisfy this void. "Turn to me and be gracious to me, for I am lonely and afflicted. The troubles of my heart are enlarged; Bring me out of my distresses" (Psalm 25:16–17). Sad to say, I had yet to experience how much crueler this world could be—a world where I thought I had lots of friends; it was those very so-called friends that hurt me beyond measure. The more the need for a friend and having someone to lean on became important to me, the more these so-called friends found it convenient to use me to find relief from their own pain. For them, I was the new kid in town and did not deserve to be treated with kindness. These girls would laugh at me and call me filthy degrading names; they would always find ways to humiliate me in front of others, no matter how much I tried to be kind to them, how much I tried to be their friend, all I ever got in return was hatred and envy. "Greater love has no one than this, that one lay down his life for his friends" (John 15:13).

At the age of eleven, I was the victim of bullying, which affected my psychological development because of derogatory and negative remarks—remarks that were out of my control. I felt lonely, depressed, and left out. I ran away from home several times to no avail. No one knew what I felt mentally and emotionally. I began to think that I was different, and not in a good way, but in a bad way. I had innocently become Satan's toy—I was young—knowing the difference between the Lord Jesus and the enemy was something that I had never been taught. I could not understand why I was singled out as such a bad girl and why was I being treated so mean? "Why are you in despair, O my soul? And why have you become disturbed within me? Hope in God, for I shall yet praise Him, The help of my countenance, and my God" (Psalm 42:11).

I can still remember there were many times with tears in my eyes, I wanted to yell and say, "Please, someone help me!" In all reality, I needed my Savior, but the knowledge of the true Savior was beyond all that I was brought up to believe in. I was raised a Catholic; I did my First Holy Communion, my Confirmation, and, finally, Holy Matrimony, but I never knew what it was like to have a personal relationship with the Lord Jesus. How I needed Him. I was blind and could not see my precious Jesus, who was standing right there in front of me with open arms. "Before I formed you in the womb, I knew you, and before you were born, I consecrated you;" (Jeremiah 1:5). He knew me; He has always been with me. So, you ask, "Then, why did He allow all the pain and shame? Why didn't He just stop it?" He did not stop it because He had a different plan. He allowed it for a good purpose, and this purpose was the salvation of many lost souls, and, in the process, it would bring honor and glory to His name.

Acceptance

The time came when I stepped into a different world, a world where I could just be me and not be criticized, judged, or marginalized—a world where I would never have to face the reality of being different from others; I would fit in now because I would now be doing the same things they were doing. Right on the same block where I lived, at the age of twelve, and with a brain that had not been fully developed yet, I was led into a deception that has been very well known to mankind, and because I wanted to be accepted, I began experimenting with different controlled substances: from sniffing spray paint—or "huffing paint," as some call it—to drinking alcohol, street drugs and everything else in-between. The enemy was out to get me and tried his best to devour me, but the Lord was watching over me. "Be of sober spirit, be on the alert. Your adversary, the devil, prowls about like a roaring lion, seeking someone to devour" (1 Peter 5:8).

I, the eldest of six children, was now unintentionally setting a bad example for my younger siblings, something that I regretted for years on end until I found peace through the saving grace and forgiveness of the Heavenly Father. The bad example that I demonstrated in front of them carried with it much guilt and condemnation.

I began to connect with others, who obviously were also battling some sort of inner torment, and because we all had issues in our personal and social environments, to us it was nothing out of the ordinary to be disobedient to our parents—from talking back to them, coming home at odd hours of the night, to losing interest for school. Around this same time, at the age of thirteen, my first consensual sexual act was consummated, and this encounter never amounted to anything except to add more shame to the shame that was already festering within me—becoming worse and more intense than ever. The worst part was that this sexual encounter was evolved around one of my drunken stupor moments, and then it dawned on me that the very same derogatory and dreaded comments that I was forced to listen to as, a child, had now become a reality; it was as if I fitted that mold perfectly. As a child, I could deny those comments, but now it was hard for me to say that the names they once hurled at me were not true. This actuality pulled me further down into a sea of misery and disgust.

For this is the will of God, your sanctification; that is, that you abstain from sexual immorality; that each of you know how to possess his own vessel in sanctification and honor, not in lustful passion, like the Gentiles who do not know God...For God has not called us for the purpose of impurity, but in sanctification.

1 Thessalonians 4:3–5, 7

Bad Choices

My transition from childhood to adulthood was a burden, it was not easy; I had run into numerous walls and jumped over many hurdles, and yet there was more to come. I was now twenty-seven years old, and the choices I made were not good; I continued to drink—I was very much an alcoholic—and had to face another moment in my life that was incredibly sad. The father of my one and only daughter, Amanda, had just passed away in a drowning accident, and it was a metaphor for the same guilt that I had gone through with my dad. Again, I felt that if I would have been there for him, this would not have happened. So, there I went again, beating myself up for something that I did not have any control over, much less having to pay the price for something that was unpreventable. I felt so down and out over his death that I was now going full force into finding whatever I could get my hands on to feel normal, and because of my vulnerability, I made it so convenient for Satan to introduce me to an opioid—a controlled substance that is very addicting. This day would go down in history for me because of the bad choice to submit to the deception of this hardcore drug, all because I was looking for a way of escape— escape from a life that I felt was not fair, a life that, from early on, I knew I had not lived well.

Therefore, through the deception of the enemy and all his workers of iniquity, this street drug grabbed a hold of me. It is one of the most aggressive evil bondages known to mankind— an illegal, highly addictive opioid drug was what I chose as a way of escape instead of choosing the Lord and His saving grace. Regardless of the bad choices that I repeatedly made, the Lord Jesus gave Satan permission to abuse and hurt me, but only for a season. "Then the Lord said to Satan, 'Behold, all that he has is in your power, only do not put forth your hand on him'" (Job 1:12).

Immediately, I began to change; I had become a victim of circumstance, once again; I was out of control this time, with a craving and a need for this opioid that words cannot express. Today, I can see the evil one saying, "Welcome to my world, you fool." I was taken on a long, horrific ride—twenty-seven years of bringing shame and disgust to my Father's temple, almost to the point of death.

"Do you not know that you are a temple of God and that the Spirit of God dwells in you? If any man destroys the temple of God, God will destroy him, for the temple of God is holy, and that is what you are" (1 Corinthians 3:16–17).

This is something which will be taking place very soon, when Jesus comes and destroys the Destroyer himself, "And the devil who deceived them was thrown into the lake of fire and brimstone, where the beast and the false prophet are also; and they will be tormented day and night forever and ever" (Revelation 20:10).

Throughout my life, I gave birth to three children—as I said earlier, my daughter Amanda, who has blessed me with my grandchildren, Damien and Abriana; and my other children—two sons, Manuel and Joseph, whom I love dearly. In my heart, I wanted to be the best mother for my children, but the choices I made caused me to fail; therefore, my mom was a mother to my children; she provided for them and nurtured them. How could I let this happen? I immediately put myself in check and took into consideration the fact that I was not close to the Lord, but open prey for Satan—this scenario, from a spiritual perspective, can have a significant impact that makes all the difference in the world—from a life of defeat to a life of victory in Jesus. Behind the scenes, I was not alone in the bad choices I made; the company I kept made matters worse. "Do not be deceived: 'Bad company corrupts good morals'" (1 Corinthians 15:33). The deceiver uses others to make it seem like you are doing the right thing. At one point, I was involved with someone that was just as bad in this addiction as I was; there was no way that he would have been able to help me or set me free from this bondage. The enemy is clever; he will use any of his tools that are necessary to keep you on the evil path to destruction and accomplish his mission—anything to hurt and kill the beloved children of God.

Within the onset of withdrawals from opioid addiction, I was enticed into trafficking this drug—a good solution to my problem, but this meant an open door for incarceration. I was setting myself up, but, at the same time, believing that I was better prepared than others and that getting caught would never happen to me. I proceeded as if I was immune to getting busted, but I was wrong. What made me think that I was different from others? You break the law, you go to jail. When convicted on my first trafficking charge, I was allowed probation; that did not work, so I was sent to the Women's Correctional Facility here in New Mexico, did my time, was released on parole, and back to jail I went. It does not pay to be stubborn. While at the county jail, I still remember asking the Lord, why? Why do I have to go back to prison again? But God, in all His wisdom, knows what is best for his children.

He knew that, in there, I would submit to Him, I would study and search the scriptures, but most of all, He knew my heart, "And God, who knows the heart, bore witness to them, giving them the Holy Spirit, just as He also did to us" (Acts 15:8).

I was released, and, again, my parole was revoked, and I received the rest of my time in prison. Jail and prison time were repetitive—the handcuffs, the shackles—but what affected me the most was my freedom. That is when I began to realize how precious freedom really is, not only physically, mentally, and emotionally, but, most importantly, spiritually!

On my last journey of being on parole (2001–2004), and looking forward to finishing this last number, there was another attack from the enemy that pierced my heart; it was the day my brother overdosed on this evil drug and died, in 2003, in a rest home, and there was the guilt again. When this heart-wrenching, devastating, unexpected thing happened to my beloved brother Raymond, it just made it harder for me to refrain from this addiction. It was a time in my life where I repeatedly blamed myself for his death; I asked God to forgive me because I felt that I could have done something, and I did not. My loving and precious God forgave me, but I could not forgive myself; therefore, I went on another mission, looking for relief from the condemnation that had me bound. "He who believes in Him is not judged; he who does not believe has been judged already because he has not believed in the name of the only begotten Son of God" (John 3:18). My surviving siblings, whom I love very much, are Reuben, David, Willie, and my sister, Arleen. I sometimes feel that they understand me better than I understand myself (smile).

Throughout this life I had chosen, I encountered many regrets, such as my health; after I had already brought myself to a point of low self-es-

teem, completely drained of life itself, I was told
that I had developed cirrhosis, and that did it.
"Let no one deceive you with empty words, for
because of these things the wrath of God comes
upon the sons of disobedience" (Ephesians 5:6).
I did not want to submit my will to God, and I
was beginning to pay the consequences. I began
to cry out. See, mentally and emotionally, I had
been crying out for so many years. Since I was a
child, and now as an adult, many times thoughts
of being a failure made their way into my mind,
with their heartless plan of crushing my spirit,
and setting me at a state of low self-esteem,
aiming at making me believe that I am worthless, and of no good to no one. Condemnation
and guilt would have loved to take their course;
depression and the fear of never amounting to
anything would have set in, but…praise God! I
have a loving Savior who intervenes just at the
right time. He helped me to acknowledge that
there is hope for a better future and that "He will
never leave me or forsake me" (Hebrews 13:5).
Back then, I never received any professional

help, much less spiritual; therefore, my pain and shame escalated. I think back at the many times I needed someone that I could talk to, someone that I could trust and share all my secrets with. I never did find a friend like that until I met Jesus. We all have a higher power, someone or something that we depend and lean on, not only when times are bad, but in the good times too. Today, Jesus is my higher power; there is no power in this whole wide world higher than that—the power of Jesus, especially the healing power of my Savior.

Healing

Healing—once the mind and heart accept it, the body will also receive it. That is why it is so important to have your mind focused on God's Word. Getting into God's Word and studying it will cleanse us from top to bottom. Having faith and believing that all things are possible with Him, honors Him, and, as quickly as we believe and have faith, it moves the hand of God, motivates Him, and gives Him pleasure to help His children. He is eagerly waiting to relieve His children from all the pain and shame that they have endured throughout their lifetime.

"Ask and it shall be given to you; seek and you shall find; knock, and it shall be opened to you. For everyone who asks receives, he who seeks finds, and to him who knocks, it shall be opened" (Matthew 7:7–8).

But, with the Lord, healing comes in many ways, for different people and different reasons. For example, for some, Jesus may choose to bring on healing instantly, and others are healed through different measures, such as the case of the blind man, where the Lord did it in two steps.

"Having said these things, he spit on the ground and made mud with the saliva. Then he anointed the man's eyes with the mud and said to him, 'Go, wash in the pool of Siloam' (which means Sent). So, he went and washed and came back seeing" (John 9:6–7).

Another example would be Lazarus being raised from the dead. Again, He did it in a different way:

But when Jesus heard it, He said, "This sickness is not unto death, but for the glory of God, that the Son of God may be glorified by it." Now Jesus loved Martha, and her sister, and Lazarus. When therefore He heard that he was

sick, He stayed then two days longer in
the place where He was.

John 11:4–6

I believe that Jesus did this on purpose, to
prove a point that God is in control, and in His
time, by His authority, He alone has the victory
over all sickness, pain, disease, and death. He
is the resurrection; He is the healer. He helps us
to acknowledge, in many ways, that we cannot
survive without Him. No matter how far or close
we are to the Lord, His love remains the same
toward all humanity.

Regardless of the outcome, we do not have
the ability to know the reasons why He allows
things to happen the way they do, and the answer to "why" is in the book of Isaiah 55:8–9,
where it reads, "'For My thoughts are not your
thoughts, neither are your ways My ways,' de-
clares the Lord. 'For as the heavens are higher
than the earth, So are My ways higher than your
ways, And My thoughts than your thoughts.'"
So, who are we to say, "God shouldn't have let

that happen" or "Why hasn't He taken care of that situation?" I, for one, was consumed with and surrounded with the pangs of hell, yet His hand was constantly upon me, saying to me, "Mary Helen, you will live and not die because I have work for you to do." My healing was on the way. It was just a matter of when I surrendered, humbled, and submitted myself to His saving grace.

I learned, from a psychological lens, that the reason for my behavior was the changes that occurred during my childhood and teenage years. The dysfunctional setting and the social environment played a significant role in where I experienced a major depressive disorder; I began to lose interest in everything and consistently focused on the bad instead of the good. I always felt unworthy of the things that the Lord Jesus had to offer. My life did not have any meaning, I had lost all hope, and I did not know which way to turn.

I unknowingly believed, at that time, that everything I did was good for me because it made me feel good, to a certain point, until reality hit me in the face, and there I was again, hurting and feeling worse than before, but this time with a strong sense of guilt eating at me from within—another tool that the enemy used to keep me steadfast in my addiction. "For my iniquities are gone over my head; As a heavy burden they weigh too much for me" (Psalm 38:4). There came a point in my life where I realized that the Lord allowed me to wander. He knew that one day, I would get tired of the life I was living, and I did. I was tired, I was miserable; I knew, deep down in my heart, that I was slowly dying; no matter how many drugs or alcohol I consumed, the physical and emotional pain was still there; I felt weak, helpless, and withdrawals would never stop. Day in and day out, every day the same thing, there was never enough.

My addiction became so bad that I was constantly on one of the main streets here in this city. Every day, I made my way to the stores to pan-handle, and if the opportunity was there, I would join others by making money illegally, making sure that I had what this body needed to feel well. I was a prisoner inside my own body; the inside of me was very weak, and I could not fight it alone. I learned, at that point, that no one else was going to be there for me when I was hurting, so making sure that I was physically and mentally able was so important.

"And although you were formerly alienated and hostile in mind, engaged in evil deeds, yet He has now reconciled you in His fleshly body through death, in order to present you before Him holy and blameless and beyond reproach" (Colossians 1:21–22).

This tedious behavior was time-consuming; I could feel my body was fatigued, exhausted, and I wanted out. I needed to start, as early as I could, to accomplish what needed to be done, by the end of the day, to be financially stable, to acquire what I needed to carry me through to the next morning and function properly throughout the day; even then, it was never enough. It is so sad to make money your number one priority, and that was what my life was all about; that is all I ever thought about. I was always scheming, always planning; if I had money left over from the night before, automatically, my mind began to calculate—it became a way of life for me. "And you were dead in your trespasses and sins, in which you formerly walked according to the course of this world, according to the prince of the power of the air, of the spirit that is now working in the sons of disobedience" (Ephesians 2:1–2).

Apart from all the self-infliction I imposed on myself, there were many people that were critical and judgmental of me. Their thoughts on what they believed about me and knowing that they could care less what happened to me would cross my mind, every now and then, but it still did not change the fact of the condition I was in, or the help that I needed; it would go in one side of my brain and come out the other way. I refused to let their negative criticism or remarks pull me down further, to begin with; I was already a negative thinking individual—living in a negative world filled with hurting and lost souls. Nevertheless, it did not stop me from the horrible mission I was on. Instead, I learned to ignore those that were in the same situation as I was and focused on using, abusing, and manipulating people—from family members, friends, and acquaintances to people I did not even know. It did not matter their age, race, or gender, and this is just a mild way of saying how far I had gotten into this dark world. Repeatedly, all I ever thought of was, *You need to feed the animal that lives within you*, and that is all that mattered. The enemy had me right where he wanted me; spiritually speaking, he taught me to think the way he thinks. "And do not be conformed to this world, but be transformed by the renewing of your mind, that you may prove what the will of God is, that which is good and acceptable and perfect" (Romans 12:2). This transformation had not taken place yet; therefore, I was vulnerable, and this made it easier for Satan to teach me how to convince, lie, and cheat whoever I approached, or whoever approached me, and they were in for a wicked and skillful manipulation, of a person that was desperate; unless they already knew the life, or they had dealt with me personally in the past, they would just look at me and walk away.

"Rejection!" O' boy, that alone did not make me feel good at all; "rejection" is something that had been hard for me to deal with for so many years, but again, I learned to brush it off and wait for the next "victim." This went on day after day. Deep down, I knew that I not only was hurting myself physically, mentally, and emotionally, but the one thing that scared me the most was that I was deeply hurting myself spiritually. I knew that if I died under these circumstances, I would go directly to hell for eternity. "The wicked will return to Sheol, Even all the nations who forget God" (Psalm 9:17). When you are a menace, a rebel, an outcast, a person thought of as worthless, a no good for nothing or nobody, you become a cold, heartless person, living only for yourself; you become so caught up in this vicious lifestyle that you also do not realize what you are putting your body through; your whole existence is decaying, and there is no acknowledgment of it until, in some cases, it is too late.

Throughout my years in prison, I met many women who were bound with the same chains but never received spiritual healing through the salvation that the Lord has to offer, much less the freedom they so desperately longed for. They never wanted anything to do with my Savior, and eventually, they died in their sins. Salvation is ours for the taking, and it comes by acknowledging the need of the Lord Jesus and His saving grace because He made a way, "And there is salvation in no one else; for there is no other name under heaven that has been given among men, by which we must be saved" (Acts 4:12).

There is much to say about healing, even when it comes to healing from our past—the unfortunate circumstances and the dishonorable choices we made. This, I would say, would be up there on top of our list because the enemy has a way of using our past to remind us of the pain and the shame that had us bound in the first place.

Dealing with the Past

My past was something that was hard for me to overcome, from the earliest memories of my childhood until now as an adult, the pain, shame, guilt, and condemnation posed as stumbling blocks—barriers that made it hard for me to stay on the right path, for example, when I was released from prison those six times, I know now that the reason I had a hard time was that I was not standing on a solid foundation, and that foundation is "Jesus." When released from prison, I did not continue studying His Word and gradually began to drift away, therefore, making it difficult for me to continue my walk with Him. All the time I spent in prison studying God's Word was for my benefit, but upon my release, I could say that it was done in vain because I was not rooted in Him.

When anyone hears the word of the kingdom, and does not understand it, the evil one comes and snatches away what has been sown in his heart. This is the one on whom seed was sown beside the road. And the one on whom seed was sown on the rocky places, this is the man who hears the word, and immediately receives it with joy; yet he has no firm root in himself, but is only temporary, and when affliction or persecution arises because of the word, immediately he falls away. "And the one on whom seed was sown among the thorns, this is the man who hears the word, and the worry of the world, and the deceitfulness of riches choke the word, and it becomes unfruitful. "And the one on whom seed was sown on the good soil, this is the man who hears the word and understands it; who indeed bears fruit, and brings forth, some a hundredfold, some sixty, and some thirty.

Matthew 13:19–23

This is only done by humbling oneself from a sincere heart—a heart that wants only what God wants, a heart that wants to bring honor and glory to His name because He alone deserves all the praise. I thank God that through His Son Jesus I was blessed with His grace (unmerited favor), a favor I did not deserve. I am so grateful for His gracious goodness, especially because of everything wrong that I did throughout my life. I praise Him every day for being my Shepherd—a Shepherd who cares dearly for His lambs, "The Lord is my Shepherd, I shall not want" (Psalm 23:1). Jesus is the only one that can enter the very core of your being and remove all forms of evil, bondages, and fear. He cuts out pieces such as selfishness, anger, bitterness, resentment, unforgiveness, and rebelliousness. What other god would do this for us? What other god would give his only Son to die on the cross for us? None other than God Almighty, the Creator of the heavens, the earth, all living creatures, and all humanity. He is the God that did all these things for us; He is the one true God that is worthy of all our praise.

Every morning, while on my knees, I ask Jesus to remove anything that is not from Him from my life. Today, beyond a shadow of a doubt, I desire with all my heart to be a daughter pleasing to my Abba Father. Of course, I am still not perfect, but there will come a day where He will finish what He started in me. "For I am confident of this very thing, that He who began a good work in you will perfect it until the day of Christ Jesus" (Philippians 1:6). Therefore, staying in right standing with Him, and manifesting a positive attitude, is mandatory to live a life that is pleasing to Him.

You are the light of the world. A city set on a hill cannot be hidden. Nor do men light a lamp, and put it under the peck-measure, but on the lampstand; and it gives light to all who are in the house. Let your light shine before men in such a way that they may see your good works, and glorify your Father who is in heaven.

Matthew 5:14–16

Self-Righteously Judgmental

Self-righteous means that we are strongly convinced of our own righteousness, in other words, that we are better than others, in more ways than one, when in all reality, we became the righteousness of the Father through what Jesus did for us, "He made Him who knew no sin to be sin on our behalf, that we might become the righteousness of God in Him" (2 Corinthians 5:21).

So, why act as if we have never done anything wrong. There are many who carry on this way; they look down on others and carry on as if they, themselves, have never done anything wrong. Then, there are those who claim to be children of God who do the same. I admit that I am guilty of doing this. I have caught myself many times speaking in a judgmental manner about others. I forgot where I had come from and began to look down on others, judging them, and talking bad about them, until the Holy Spirit began to work in my life by convicting me and showing me that the same things I would say about others, I, too, was demonstrating the very same acts. "Therefore you are without excuse, every man of you who passes judgment, for in that you judge another, you condemn yourself; for you who judge practice the same things" (Romans 2:1). The Bible warns us not to use our spiritual freedom for selfish purposes: "For you were called to freedom, brethren; only do not turn your freedom into an opportunity for the flesh, but through love serve one another" (Galatians 5:13).

So, then, when I became self-righteously judgmental, I, in all reality, was taking advantage of my salvation—of my spiritual freedom—by carrying on as if I never knew what it was to do wrong, and gradually, it became a sin. When we start to point fingers at others, we need to immediately put ourselves in check; we have no place whatsoever to judge anyone. In the book of John, it says, "For not even the Father judges anyone, but He has given all judgment to the Son" (John 5:22). This becomes just as bad as idolizing oneself when we put ourselves in the Lord's position. "Judge not, that you be not judged" (Matthew 7:1).

Idolatry

Biblically, idolatry is to worship other things instead of the one true God. It became a major influence back in the Old Testament times, and it still has the same influence on us today.

You shall not make for yourself and idol, or any likeness of what is in heaven above or on the earth beneath or in the water under the earth. "You shall not worship them or serve them; for I, the Lord your God, am a jealous God, visiting the iniquity of the fathers on the children, on the third and the fourth generations of those who hate Me, but showing lovingkindness to thousands to those who love Me and keep My commandments.

Exodus 20:4–6

Over and over, the Word of God mentions that idolatry is wrong. These gods are made of metals, such as gold and silver. Some were made of wood or stone, but whatever they were made of, they were powerless material things. Worshipping idols is an abomination to the Lord. "Therefore, my beloved, flee from idolatry" (1 Corinthians 10:14).

To trust in idols is to remove God from His place of exaltation and exalting other things that are not worthy of our praise. These gods disguise themselves; they hide behind things that you would never suspect, such as food, money, lust, illegal and prescription drugs, alcohol, cars, power, fame, pornography—anything that a person idolizes is idolatry. They take God's place. I innocently idolized money, lust, drugs, alcohol, and cars, and I say innocently because, at that time, I was ignorant of God's Word; therefore, idolatry to me was something that I became familiar with as I studied the Word. We, as people that have been involved or are now involved with some types of addiction, are guilty of idolatry. "And when the multitudes saw what Paul had done, they raised their voice, saying in the Lycaonian language, "The gods have become like men and have come down to us" (Acts 14:11). This multitude of people were into idolatry so much that when Paul, through the Holy Spirit, spoke to a man that was lame and he was healed immediately, they thought their gods, the ones they idolized, had come down in the flesh. This reveals how distorted their minds were; does that sound familiar? Instead of worshipping the Son of God, who did come in the flesh, they worshipped and idolized gods that could not do what Jesus could do for them. These gods could not heal their bodies or supply all their needs, but, most of all, these gods could not pay the price for their sins. What a terrible mistake they were led to believe, but then again, such are the lives of humanity today. They did not reach this point by mere coincidence; someone had to have taught them this way of belief. Again, does this sound familiar?

"Gather yourselves and come; draw near together, you fugitives from the nations. They have no knowledge, Who carry about their wooden idol, And pray to a god who cannot save" (Isaiah 45:20).

We can also put people on a pedestal by paying too much attention to them or by always trying to impress them—they become the center of everything we do. We lose focus on what really matters, especially our souls. Therefore, anything or anyone that becomes a god in our lives becomes our idol.

> Or do you not know that the unrighteous shall not inherit the kingdom of God? Do not be deceived; neither fornicators, nor idolaters, nor adulterers, nor effeminate, nor homosexuals, nor thieves, nor the covetous, nor drunk-

ards, nor revilers, nor swindlers, shall inherit the kingdom of God.

1 Corinthians 6:9–10

This is just one of God's warnings. There are numerous scriptures that warn against idol worshipping. Search the scriptures.

Who is the mastermind and instigator of all this idolatry? Well, his name is "Satan," and he has been around from the very beginning, deceiving, and misguiding the children of the one true God. The enemy has no remorse, never has, never will; he slithered his way into humanity, and if given permission by the Almighty, Satan will take us on an adventure to places where we will find ourselves at a point of no return—another reason to stay close to the Father. Granted, the Lord, for various reasons, and for a good purpose, allows Satan to toy with us, but He also provides a way of escape, "No temptation has overtaken you but such as is common to man; and God is faithful, who will not allow you to be tempted beyond what you are able, but with the temptation will provide the way of escape also, that you may be able to endure it" (1 Corinthians 10:13). Satan can care less who we are, our age, our identity, what our nationality is, who our families are, our employment, our education, etc. His main purpose is to destroy the kingdom and children of God. Some, by putting their trust in this false god, have been taken out of this world into eternal damnation because of either the lack of knowledge between the one true God and the false god or just plain being stubborn. Satan is evil and not to be trusted.

On the other hand, the one true God is a God who can be trusted. He has, for many generations, kept His word to His people and is very much a gentleman. He does not push Himself on us or force us to follow His commands. He leaves it up to us to heed His warning, and if that is not enough, then we set ourselves up for a life of misery and pain. Jesus says, "I am the vine, you are the branches; he who abides in Me, and I in him, he bears much fruit; for apart from Me you can do nothing" (John 15:5). He is the only one who will lead us in the right direction and helps us to make the right choices. He is the omniscient God who knows all things. He is omnipotent, all-powerful, and omnipresent—is everywhere at the same time. To exclude Him out of our lives would bring unhappiness and corruption into our world. He created the heavens and the earth; He created you and me—we are His children.

"For God so loved the world that He gave His only begotten Son, that whosoever believes in Him should not perish, but have eternal life" (John 3:16). We cannot find a love like that in something that is made from silver or gold.

> But our God is in the heavens; He does whatever He pleases. Their idols are silver and gold, The work of man's hands. They have mouths, but they cannot speak; they have eyes, but they cannot see; They have ears, but cannot hear; They have noses, but they cannot smell; They have hands, but they cannot feel;

They have feet, but they cannot walk;
They cannot make a sound with their
throat. Those who make them will become like them, Everyone who trusts in
them.

Psalm 115:3–8

Only the Son, Jesus Christ, the one who shed His blood on Calvary, can set us free. He is the God of love. His name is Wonderful Counselor, Almighty God, Eternal Father, and the Prince of Peace. There is nothing too hard for Him.

If we, as a nation, had more insight on this subject, there would not be so much violence and chaos in this world. It is sad to say that the knowledge of the one true God and everything concerning Him has become a "hush-hush" thing in our society. His name cannot be mentioned in some schools, at our jobs, and when the question of who the higher power is at an N.A. meeting, you cannot mention the name of Jesus. What has our world come to? Now, in 2022, will we be a generation that turns completely to God, or will we continue idolizing other things that will bring forth corruption?

We all, as individuals, will be given the opportunity someday, somewhere, somehow, to choose whom we will serve. Will it be the false god, the "evil one," or the true God, the one who loves us unconditionally, the one who will never leave us or forsake us. Truly, having the knowledge on which God we serve will ultimately make a difference in the way we live our lives, and in our eternal destiny. Our ultimate goal should be to have faith, believe, and pray. Praying is basically talking to God. He knows us personally. The mindset of your heart, your honesty: this is what counts the most. Open your heart and let Him know how much you need Him, no matter what you are struggling with. I have never forgotten this one time in my life when I was all upset with an ex-boyfriend, I angrily barked at him, "Why didn't you do what I asked of you?" He said, "You never asked me to do this for you," and then, I remembered, he was right. He then proceeded to say, "Always remember a closed mouth don't get fed." So, the point I am making is that the same goes with our Father—He loves when His children open up and pray and converse with Him, but if we do not open our mouths, we will not get fed. Especially when it comes to the salvation of our souls or the souls of our loved ones. "'Come now, and let us reason together,' says the Lord, 'Though your sins are as scarlet, They will be as white as snow; Though they are red like crimson, They will be like wool'" (Isaiah 1:18). The first prayer that a person should say when they want to get right with Jesus and receive Him as their personal Lord and Savior is the Sinner's Prayer. It goes like this: "In the name of Jesus, Father, I am sorry for all the wrong things I have done in my life. Thank you for dying on the cross for me and setting me free from all my transgressions and forgiving me. Please, come into my heart and lead me and guide me all the days of my life, in Your name, I pray, Jesus, Amen." From the beginning of the Bible, a sincere prayer has always touched the very heart of God.

The Lord's Prayer

The Lord's prayer taught to us by the Lord Jesus Himself is a good place to start. It starts off by saying, "our," and the reason for this word is that when Jesus was teaching His disciples the Lord's Prayer, He not only included Himself in the prayer to the Father, but He also included all of us as well. "Our" meaning Him (Jesus) and His disciples, and since we accepted Jesus as our Savior, we too become His disciples. Jesus is revealing to us that the Father is not only His Father, but He is our Father too.

"Pray, then, in this way: Our Father who art in heaven, Hallowed be thy name" (Matthew 6:9). The beginning of this prayer has much meaning and value to the Father because of the reverence demonstrated by those who are called His children—these children reveal the respect that He alone deserves; we address Him as our Father because we now know that we are a part of His family, and we have a special place in His heart—so special that at the beginning of this prayer, it opens the doors of heaven, and there, we find the assurance that He has placed us in a secure place. "Keep me as the apple of the eye; Hide me in the shadow of Thy wings" (Psalm 17:8). Praise our Savior Jesus! for being an obedient Son, for making a way for us to have this personal relationship with the Father, and without a doubt, "Casting all your anxiety upon Him, because He cares for you" (1 Peter 5:7). I, personally, experience such a wonderful peace just knowing that I do have a Father—a Heavenly Father; a Father that I can confide in, and with confidence tell Him, "Here you go, Dad, take care of this for me," and in the process enjoy His peace, amen?

"Thy kingdom come. Thy will be done, On earth as it is in heaven" (Matthew 6:10). We stand firm and depend on His Word and know that what He says will come to pass because who can distort the will of God? No one that I know of! God is in control forever until the end of time. His will be done on earth, just like it is in heaven, and nothing or no one can change that. I am looking forward to the day when:

> And He shall wipe away every tear from their eyes; and there shall no longer be any death; there shall no longer be any mourning, or crying, or pain; the first things have passed." And He who sits on the throne said, "Behold, I am making all things new." And He said, "Write, for these words are faithful and true." "And He said to me, "It is done. I am the Alpha and the Omega, the beginning and the end. I will give to the one who thirsts from the spring of the water of life without cost.
>
> Revelation 21:4–6

This is just a reminder, folks, that we must stay true to our Father with a thankful heart for the wisdom that He has blessed us with so that we may someday enjoy these fruits because Satan will have us believe otherwise. Speaking for myself, when the enemy entices or tempts me, and I know now that it is against my Father's will, I have the right, as God's child, to rebuke him and ask him to leave because everything that the enemy has set before me in the past has been straight up a trap. If there is one thing that the enemy has always hoped for, it is that I had never discovered that I have the God-given right to stop his plans and movements. But I do know now, thanks to the Holy Spirit, the teacher, the one who teaches me all things. Yes, I sure did use my God-given authority, and I rebuked Satan and all his lies. I put my foot down, called up to heaven in a very frustrated way, and said these words, "Lord Jesus, help me! Can't You hear me, Lord? I need help! I want to stop all this; I am tired of this life."

Obviously, I could not stop it on my own, and no one in this world had the power to set me free; no one could remove the chains except Jesus. He heard my cry and delivered me from all my addictions, just like David cried out,

> I waited patiently for the Lord; And He inclined to me, and heard my cry. He brought me up out of the pit of destruction, out of the miry clay; And He set my feet upon a rock making my footsteps firm. And He put a new song in my mouth, a song of praise to our God; Many will see and fear, and will trust in the Lord.
>
> Psalm 40:1–3

He has given me a new song to sing praises to my God, amen.

"Give us this day our daily bread" (Matthew 6:11). Our daily bread is all our needs for that day. We must depend on Him to deliver those needs because He is our provider, in whom we trust. I learned the hard way that staying connected to God was the best thing that I could do. I had been a fool too long, and I had lost for too long and needed to get back on track and claim everything that belonged to me, back from the enemy. I needed to stop feeling sorry for myself and stop saying, "I can't do this," and instead say, "I have the victory in Jesus!" I can do all things through Him. I needed to put on the full armor of my Father, which is part of my daily bread for the day, and stand my ground and show Satan that I now have the armor of God on. "No weapon that is formed against you shall prosper; And every tongue that accuses you in judgment you will condemn" (Isaiah 54:17). The Holy Spirit, the teacher, helped me to realize that the enemy does not have any power over me anymore. The Comforter said, "You are God's child"—His temple where He dwells.

Once our eyes are opened to this, eventually, we begin to get stronger in our walk with Him. We notice that the things we once thought we could not let go of—things that once seemed so important to us—will now be the things that we now care the least about. Paul tells us,

> But whatever things were gain to me, those things I have counted as loss for the sake of Christ. More than that, I count all things to be loss in view of the surpassing value of knowing Christ Jesus my Lord, for whom I have suffered the loss of all things, and count them but rubbish in order that I may gain Christ,
>
> Philippians 3:7–8

As I have grown closer to my Heavenly Father, these things have no meaning at all. The things I once did, the things that were the highlight of my day, have now become such a sad and filthy life, especially watching the very same people that I connected with still in bondage. Not only has He changed the way I think, the way I talk, the things I do, but He has also changed the desires of my heart. "And my God shall supply all your needs according to His riches in glory in Christ Jesus" (Philippians 4:19).

"And forgive us our debts, as we also have forgiven our debtors" (Matthew 6:12). Through Jesus, God the Father most gladly forgives us, when we ask and repent—by turning away from our sins and walking the other way—that is truly repenting! Sometimes, giving up the old way of life can be hard to do, but with God's help, all things are possible. We need to daily remember that to receive our Father's loving forgiveness, we too must forgive others and ourselves. "Forgiveness is unlocking the door to set someone free and realizing you were the prisoner" (author: unknown). When unforgiveness has its way in a person's life, it causes many problems, not only with the other person but with God Himself. To forgive is one of God's commands, not doing so will ruin your relationship with Him and cause it to never flourish. "And be kind to one another, tender-hearted, forgiving each other; just as God in Christ also has forgiven you" (Ephesians 4:32). Besides, carrying around a grudge will cause us more harm than good—with it comes jealousy, anger, frustration, bitterness, also feelings of revenge, which then bring on retaliation. The devil, of course, will try to convince us that if we are still having ill feelings toward the individual that hurt us, we never truly forgave them; no! Forgiving and still feeling the same way is only natural; we're human! I believe that there is not one person in this world that can forgive, forget, and be jolly and cheery; now, that would be inhumane! But, as long as we do our part like God wants us to, then He will do the rest in His time. God has the power to change the way we feel towards those who hurt us; we just need to trust Him—He will do it!

Making the decision to forgive others is not all there is; the job is not finished yet. Our Father says, "But I say to you, love your enemies, and pray for those who persecute you" (Matthew 5:44). We are showing mercy to those who do not deserve it. Think about it: our Lord and Savior did and does the same for us; therefore, having mercy on others would be the right thing to do in God's eyes, don't you think? Besides, we have a Helper who will help us because we cannot really forgive without help from the Holy Spirit. So, we need to remember to pray before we proceed, and ask the Holy Spirit to breathe on us, and give us the strength and a humble heart to forgive and to bless that person who hurt us. When we obey our Father and find it in our hearts to forgive others, it becomes a release from anxiety and distress because not only are we set free, but through our obedience, we set the person that hurt us free.

Again, speaking from experience, when I dedicated my life back to my Savior, I began to forgive all those that had done me wrong—since my birth—as far back as I can remember until now, and I even asked God to remind me of the ones that I had forgotten to forgive, and believe me He will bring them to your remembrance— like I said earlier, "All we have to do is ask, and He is more than happy to help us. He helps us by sending us the Holy Spirit who is our Helper (John 14:16), our Teacher (1 Corinthians 2:13), our Guide (John 16:13), our Comforter, and our Counselor (John 14:16); God makes sure that we do not have any excuse when it comes to doing His will. He supplies us with every tool that is needed to get the job done, believe that! We do not serve a God who is on the late bus, and to think that He provides all these things for us, for our own good, so that we can be at peace with Him and live a life that is pleasing to Him. He loves us dearly and, someday, we will reach that point where we will be perfect inside and out, and that is a promise! God's Word says it: "Therefore you are to be perfect, as your Heavenly Father is perfect" (Matthew 5:48).

"And do not lead us into temptation, but deliver us from evil. [For thine is the kingdom and the power and the glory, forever. Amen.]" (Matthew 6:13). Check this out, the devil knows our weaknesses, and trust me, he will use them against us. But hey, there is a way out!

See, it is our weaknesses, not our strengths, that draw us closer to God. "And He has said to me, My grace is sufficient for you, for power is perfected in weaknesses. Most gladly, therefore, I will rather boast about my weaknesses, that the power of Christ may dwell in me" (2 Corinthians 12:9). Even if we do not admit that we are weak, our human strength still cannot set us free. Only by God's grace can we have the power to overcome the evil one because the kingdom, the power, and the glory are His forever, and there is not one person in this world or any demon in hell that can ever take that away from Him—He is the all-powerful God, even over the enemy of our souls.

The Enemy

There is a burden that, in many cases, is indescribably hard to set aside; this burden is the burden of the mind, when thoughts of regret, thoughts of confusion, feelings of deep sorrow caused by loss or disappointment get the best of us, it does not leave us alone; it is constantly badgering us, especially in the quiet moments of our lives. We begin to condemn ourselves, in some cases not enough to commit suicide, but just enough to cause us to turn to the world, to find the comfort we are hungering and aching for. The questions that run through our minds are, Why? Why did this happen to me? Why did that happen to them? Why do I have to endure the pain and shame of a life not lived well? Why, why, why? The answer is the enemy, the father of all lies. When we were serving the enemy, because that is what we were doing—we were fulfilling his desires, we were straight-up deceived by the Liar himself. Jesus said of him,

> You are of your father the devil, and you want to do the desires of your father. He was a murderer from the beginning, and does not stand in the truth, because there is no truth in him. Whenever he speaks a lie, he speaks from his own nature; for he is a liar, and the father of lies.
>
> John 8:44

Therefore, through the enemy's deception, we became enemies of God. But…through the grace of God, there are some of us that know who the enemy is, and there are probably some who are reading this book that do not know or who have never been interested in finding out who the enemy is, but for the purpose of acknowledging why things happen the way they do—hardships, trials, tribulations, wars, mental, emotional, physical pain, and death—we need to be aware and alert at all times that our enemy is "Satan." He is against God and all of God's children, which is every created being that has ever lived and is living now, especially those who have put their trust in God. The enemy has a clever way of hiding his malicious plans—he manipulates God's plans to enhance his because of his jealousy and hatred of the loving Father of lights and because of the retaliation that lingers within him; he cannot and never will accept the fact that the Almighty God removed him from His presence.

> Son of man, take up a lamentation over the king of Tyre, and say to him, 'Thus says the Lord God, "You had the seal of perfection, Full of wisdom and perfect in beauty. "You were in Eden, the garden of God; The ruby, the topaz, and the diamond; The beryl, the onyx, and the jasper; The lapis lazuli, the turquoise, and the emerald; and the gold, the work-

manship of your settings and sockets, Was in you. On the day that you were created They were prepared. "You were the anointed cherub who covers, And I placed you there. You were on the holy mountain of God; You walked in the midst of the stones of fire. "You were blameless in ways From the day you were created, Until unrighteousness was found in you. "By the abundance of your trade You were internally filled with violence, And you sinned; Therefore I have cast you as profane From the mountain of God. And I have destroyed you, O covering cherub, From the midst of the stones of fire. "Your heart was lifted up because of your beauty; You corrupted your wisdom by reason of your splendor. I cast you to the ground; I put you before kings, That they may see you. "By the multitude of your iniquities, In the unrighteousness of your trade, You profaned your sanctuaries. Therefore I have brought fire from the midst of you; It has consumed you, And I have turned you to ashes on the earth In the eyes of all who see you. "All who know you among the peoples Are appalled at you; You have become terrified, And you will be no more.

Ezekiel 28:12–19

Now that we know who Satan is, where he came from, and where he dwells, which is right here on earth, where do we stand? Well, we stand right where God has placed us, right where God wants us. When an individual is active and doing God's will, nothing in this life happens or comes to pass by coincidence, as some believe. So, to guard ourselves against the enemy, we need to be in right standing with the Creator. How? By accepting His Son Jesus as our personal Lord and Savior, by reading His Word and standing on His promises. Why? Because Satan's attacks are nothing to play with, these attacks are called fiery darts, but the Lord has provided the shield of faith that guards us against these darts—darts such as serious health issues, losing a loved one, losing a job because of lies, struggling against some form of addiction, worrying about a rebellious child, discrimination, racism, or a spouse that is interested in some type of sexual immorality, etc. Regardless of the attack, your weapon is the shield of faith. "In addition to all, taking up the shield of faith with which you will be able to extinguish all the flaming missiles of the evil one" (Ephesians 6:16). Keep in mind that the main ingredient in this scripture is "faith," you must totally have faith and trust our Father, who promises to provide for us when these attacks are out of our control, and through His precious Holy Spirit, we will have the victory over the enemy.

Jesus knew what we would need to have the power to live a life pleasing to Him, and this power comes through the Holy Spirit, a sweet person that is irresistible when it comes to having a friend to lean on—a person that you can rely on to fulfill all that is required of a child of the Almighty God.

Holy Spirit

I am thankful that Jesus sends the Holy Spirit to those who accept Him as their personal Lord and Savior. Jesus says to His followers,

And I will ask the Father, and He will give you another Helper, that He may be with you forever; that is the Spirit of truth, whom the world cannot receive, because it does not behold Him or know Him, but you know Him because He abides with you and will be in you. "I will not leave you as orphans; I will come to you.

John 14:16–18

The filling of the Holy Spirit is God's gift to mankind; He eagerly waits for that one humble soul who is willing and waiting to do all that pleases God. "But the Helper, the Holy Spirit, whom the Father will send in My name, He will teach you all things, and bring to your remembrance all that I said to you" (John 14:26). Listen, my brothers and sisters, the Holy Spirit is our teacher, who reveals to us all things concerning our Father from above. He is our Helper in times of trouble, He is our voice when we cry out to the Lord, and our voice when we speak and demonstrate through our actions, to a lost world, that we are an example of the Lord Jesus Christ, which many times actions do speak louder than words.

Therefore, carrying ourselves in a proper and respectful way will come naturally when we depend on the guidance of the precious Holy Spirit, especially in this world where there are, at this day and time, numerous lost souls—souls that are headed directly for hell. He also is our power to resist all temptations. The Holy Spirit guides us in the right direction and comforts us when we are feeling down. He cries with us, laughs with us. He never talks bad about us or humiliates us in front of others; instead, He lifts us up and encourages us. He does not have to go out of His way to talk to us. He takes pleasure and enjoys conversing with us because of the love He has for us as children of God. He never forces us to do anything because He has proven Himself to be a gentleman so many times.

Speaking for myself, having a true friend had been one of my greatest needs, and Jesus met that need by supplying the most wonderful and trustworthy friend in the whole wide world, the Holy Spirit.

Without the leading of the Holy Spirit, I could have never lifted myself up out of the rut of damnation; it was His conviction that led me to the foot of the cross, where I found the mercy and grace that I did not deserve, and the love of a Savior by the name of "Jesus" who, by his unconditional love, grabbed a hold of me and pulled me out of the grave. The Word says, "For

Thou has delivered my soul from death, Indeed my feet from stumbling, So that I may walk before God In the light of the living" (Psalm 56:13).

Jesus did not give up on me, He did not condemn or judge me. He gave me a reason to live. He exalted me, above all that I ever could have imagined. He has opened doors for me that I thought could never be opened and has set me in high places. God says, "Because he has loved Me, therefore I will deliver him; I will set him securely on high, because he has known My name" (Psalm 91:14). He has proven to me time and time again that He was, and is, always with me, no matter how dangerous and corrupt my life had become, or the many times I felt so alone, my Savior was always there with me. "When you pass through the waters, I will be with you; And through the rivers, they will not overflow you. When you walk through fire, you will not be scorched, Nor will the flame burn you" (Isaiah 43:2). What an amazing Father!

The Holy Spirit used God's Word to help me acknowledge the truth, and it did set me free, not only from the world's prison system but from spiritual shackles that the enemy used to keep me bound. He set me free from the bondage of alcohol and drugs and released me from many sorrows, all my suffering, pain, and shame. He healed the little girl who felt so alone and confused.

Knowing Him

As strange as it may seem, it was in prison—a prison cell—where I acquired an intimate relationship with Jesus. This is where lockup time became a place of spiritual restoration for me. Yes, I studied His Word daily, but there would still be days ahead when He would still have to work within the rebelliousness of my heart—a heart that had grown cold throughout the years. I had become a bitter and selfish person.

Pursue peace with all men, and the sanctification without which no one will see the Lord. See to it that no one comes short of the grace of God; that no root of bitterness springing up causes trouble, and by it many be defiled;

Hebrews 12:14–15

Bitterness is contagious!

I never realized the way my life was affecting others, and I am not specifying loved ones. My life was affecting everyone I encountered. Without remorse, but unintentionally, I was spiritually directing them straight to eternal doom.

> But whoever causes one of these little ones who believe in Me to stumble, it is better for him that a heavy millstone be hung around his neck, and that he be drowned in the depth of the sea. Woe to the world because of its stumbling blocks! For it is inevitable that stumbling blocks come; but woe to that man through whom the stumbling block comes!
>
> Matthew 18:6–7

Through His grace, I escaped that judgment!

His Word has a positive, significant impact on those who study and meditate on the scriptures. Staying focused on His Word has taught me and still today teaches me about who my God really is, His love, authority, power, righteousness, and His justice. Knowing Him is to our advantage and the key that opens the door to His grace. How many of us, when we want to know about a celebrity, sports figure, musician, inventor, or serial killer, reach out and search for ways to find out everything about them? I can relate to that. For many of us today, we get all the information by doing research, through the media, and the rest of us get it through books—maybe an autobiography—an account of a person's life written by that person; you then purchase that book. Well, the same goes for getting to know the Creator, the Almighty Father, the *I Am*, and His Son Jesus; you go out and purchase a copy of His Word, the Bible. The moment you dig deep into the scriptures of the most famous book in the world, you will begin to see life from a different perspective. I, from experience, guarantee it! Your whole outlook on life will seem as if you are already walking on those streets of gold. Freedom! Yes!

The more I study the Bible, the more comfortable I feel when I need to express myself, especially in times of trials, tests, tribulations, or crucial circumstances that are too personal to share with others but feel safe and open to share with Him. We cannot hide anything from Him, He already knows what we need before we even say a word, "Therefore do not be like them; for your Father knows what you need, before you ask Him" (Matthew 6:8). Reading the Bible has a way of opening a person's eyes, especially the eyes of one's heart, and it cleanses us from all unrighteousness; but the washing must start from the inside out—you can change jobs, buy brand new clothes, change your cologne or perfume, and still have the same attitude and ugliness until you begin a spiritual washing from the inside out, and then people will start to see a brand new person, a person filled with God's glory and compassion, regardless of the new outfit! Jesus says, "Woe to you, scribes and Pharisees, hypocrites! For you are like whitewashed tombs which on the outside appear beautiful, but inside they are full of dead men's bones and all uncleanness" (Matthew 23:27). Deception hides behind smiling faces—behind these faces are the very fires of hell. They portray and promise a life of pleasure but are waiting to drag you to a place of torment. "Misery loves company."

On this journey with the Lord and getting to know Him more and more as the days go by, I have learned that there will be many molehills that I must jump over, and mountains that I must climb, and the only way that I would persevere and find peace for my soul would be through the process of letting go of the need to control things—because wanting to be in control was a major problem when it came to my addiction to controlled substances—and, instead, accepting the only one that could set me free.

Upon my surrendering my life to the Lord, I began to hang on to my Father's Word with everything I had and called out to Him with a pleading heart, and He began to remove from within me the trash that had accumulated throughout my life and filled it with all that is required to live a life pleasing to Him. "But He said, 'The things impossible with men are possible with God'" (Luke 18:27).

Through my precious Lord and Savior Jesus Christ, getting to know the Father has become so real to me—He has become my true source of peace, my everlasting joy, the song within my heart, my unconditional love, my Heavenly Father who has provided for me and taken care of me all the days of my life. My Father and I are one, His presence is always with me, and He helps me in my everyday tasks by supplying all my needs and offering His support and advice when it comes to dealing with my day-to-day failures and the heartbreaking consequences of my past sins.

Listen, no matter what we must go through, such as times that can be so frustrating, we must always keep in mind and remember not to get all bent out of shape over the small stuff because, by God's grace, we will be able to handle it, and at the end come out wiser, and have total victory!

Getting to know the Almighty God, I have come to realize that He can bring good out of any bad situation because He dwells within us; we have the ability to overcome. "You are from God, little children, and have overcome them; because greater is He who is in you than he who is in the world" (1 John 4:4). While getting to know Him, we must also keep in mind that there are different doctrines—other ideas or beliefs that we must stay away from, therefore, keeping to God's holy Word, the Bible, which is the very Word of our Father. Our enemy will always try his best to get our eyes off the Truth, and the Truth is Jesus: "Jesus said to him, 'I am the way, and the truth, and the life; no one comes to the Father, but through Me'" (John 14:6).

When I confessed all my sins to Him and asked Him to come and live in my heart and be my Lord and Savior, He set me free from all bondages, sicknesses, diseases, and poverty. He has been so good to me there is no way that I can fool anyone, much less Him, that I am truly not His; my very fruits testify that I am truly a child of the Most High God. He knows who are really His, Timothy put it this way, "Nevertheless, the firm foundation of God stands, having this seal, 'The Lord knows who are His,' and, 'Let everyone who names the name of the Lord abstain from wickedness'" (2 Timothy 2:19).

So, if I call myself a Christian, I cannot be doing things that are against God; what kind of witness would I be, going around from here to there, toying around with sin as I once did? To avoid the aftermath of making the same mistakes again, I have submitted my will to Him and have humbled myself to receive the rewards He has for me. So that when I stand in the day of judgment, God will look at me and say, "I am so proud of you, my daughter." "His master said to him, 'Well done, good and faithful slave; you were faithful with a few things, I will put you in charge of many things, enter into the joy of your master'" (Matthew 25:21). Today, I am a daughter who is pleasing to her Father. I am not perfect yet, but I am not the same woman who was at one time condemned to hell for worshipping and idolizing the works of the evil one.

As of this moment, I am nine years and ten months clean, and sober, and going strong, healthy as can be. Since I sincerely rededicated my life back to the Lord, I, now, at a later age, decided to go back to school; what an amazing Father! These past six years have been a long haul regarding my education, but in the process of my withdrawing from this tedious addiction, thoughts of getting an education were always tugging at my heart, which brings me here today. Because of God's love, grace, and mercy, I received two associate degrees: one in Human Services and the other in Liberal Arts in August of 2018 and along with that, two certificates: one in General Studies and the other as a substance abuse counselor—I received those in May 2021 from Central New Mexico Community College. I continued my education at New Mexico Highlands University, where I received my bachelor's in Social Work in May of 2021, a goal that had been long overdue. I attend Healing Waters Ministry, a wonderful church where I fellowship with a wonderful family of believers. Hey, fellowshipping is a must! Amen? "For the Lord is good; His lovingkindness is everlasting, And His faithfulness to all generations" (Psalm 100:5).

Conclusion

So, with all that being said, let us get to the main character of this testimonial, let us get to the purpose of this book—the purpose of this book is not for the reader to dwell on my past, the things I did or did not do. Granted, these things were a significant part of my testimony, but it was all used and revealed to bring honor and glory to His name. Our focus must stay on the one who makes it possible for us to live, the one that saves us, the one that delivers us from all things that had or have us bound, things that want to stop us from doing His work and serving Him, but, most importantly, things that want to rob us of our salvation and our eternal life with Him. Let us exalt the one true God, the God of love, mercy, forgiving and full of grace God—

the God that sent His only begotten Son "Jesus" to set humanity free—free from the pangs of hell.

God clearly spoke to me one day when I thought about publishing this book; as I stated earlier, I was struggling with doubts of writing this book and sharing my past—because of the pain and especially the shame. At that moment, the Holy Spirit saved the day! He said, "Acknowledge the truth, speak the truth, there are so many others that have gone through or are going through what you experienced and struggled with, and by you sharing your testimony, you will help them to find freedom from their despair—their complete loss and absence of hope."

Therefore, for the purpose of exalting His name, I most gladly shared how the enemy throughout my lifetime crushed me with many sorrows, especially when I recently received the bad news that I had Covid, a sorrow that no one expects would ever happen. My life was one of so much sickness and weakness; there were several times that I sat in front of my computer throughout the healing process of this evil virus trying to finish the publication of this book, and I couldn't even think straight. This virus is a monster; it affects every part of a person's body from the top of your head to the bottom of your feet, but God in all His mercy said, "Mary Helen, you will not die but live." He placed a rainbow right in front of my eyes, His way of telling me, "This will never happen again" (Genesis 9:11). You see, the Lord takes good care of His children; He did not let the evil one destroy me; He embraced me in His glory. The point that I am making here is that regardless of the negative circumstances or how painful the situation may be, don't ever forget that nothing is too big or too hard for the Almighty God.

Through His grace and mercy, no matter what you are going through, what you are having to put up with, or how tired you are from a life not lived well, we all have a way of escape—a way of escape that only Jesus can provide.

There are so many hurting people in this world. When I was blind, I couldn't see it, but now that my eyes have been opened, I can see the devastation of what this world and all the lies that come with it can do to a person; I see it everywhere. The compassion I have for the lost can be overwhelming. I just want to help everyone and let them know just how much the Savior loves them.

Brothers and sisters, you are precious to God.

Since you are precious in My sight, Since you are honored and I love you, I will give other men in your place and other peoples in exchange for your life. "Do not fear, for I am with you; I will bring your offspring from the east, And gather you from the west. "I will say to the north, 'Give them up!' And to the south, 'Do not hold them back.' Bring My sons from afar, And My daughters from the ends of the earth, Everyone who is called by My name, And whom I have created for My glory, Whom I have formed, even whom I have made.

Isaiah 43:4–7